MW00946029

THE ART OF *untangling*

MINDFULNESS JOURNAL

FOR HEALING AND TRANSFORMATION

JOANNA CIOLEK

ISBN: 1545341826
ISBN-13: 978-1545341827

You too have the power
and ability
to rise from the darkness
and unleash your greatness

Dedicated to all those committed to emotional healing, body-mind wellbeing, and genuine transformation.

THE PATH OF AWAKENING

YOU ARE HERE NOW

Hello and welcome, I'm glad you are here. Congratulate yourself. By picking up this journal you've taken the first step towards genuine change. It takes enormous strength and courage to be willing to look truth in the eye, and dare to ask more of and for yourself.

Taking responsibility for your own happiness is key to positive transformation. Well-being and fulfillment don't just happen to us - clear intention and persistent action are both necessary in order to create the kind of life we want for ourselves.

But in order to understand where you are going, you have to know where you are now. You have to look deep within, untangle your mental knots, heal old wounds, and let your intuition and inner wisdom guide you forward.

This journal will help you develop a deeper understanding of who you are and what you want for yourself, so that you can start designing a life that's truly yours!

WRITING TO HEAL AND GROW

Whether you're new to journaling or have kept a journal your entire life, it's important to recognize the healing and transformative powers of writing, especially writing in the state of mindfulness.

Writing can be a therapeutic experience of self-discovery. Journaling allows us to build an intimate relationship with ourselves, and connect with our inner world in an authentic way. Whether we're writing our gratitude list, or reaching for our journal when we're hurting, we are reconnecting with our true self, our strengths and core values, our deep feelings and emotions in that moment.

When we write we give our internal world a voice. We slow down and clear our head, and gradually deepen our understanding of ourselves. We are then able to process and make sense of what's happening with us and around us. We gain a new perspective, discover new choices, develop new mindset.

Writing gives us permission to release. By putting our fears and hurts down on paper, we can let them go without judgment or worry. Our journal becomes a safe space for us to free ourselves, get unstuck, move forward. When we write we release, and when we release we heal.

This journal is about harnessing the powers of mindfulness while writing. Mindful journaling is a meditative form of writing. When we combine writing with mindful check-ins, we learn to move our attention inward, in the spirit of curiosity, gentleness and self-compassion. We go deep within to face our fears and hang-ups head on – instead of getting entangled in them – knowing we have the inner strength and courage to overcome them, thus regaining power over how we experience and respond to life.

Mindful journaling allows us to open the lines of communication and start an honest conversation with ourselves, not from a place of self-criticism and judgment, but from a place of love and nurture.

Journaling in the spirit of mindfulness is the road to genuine transformation. This practice will allow you to show up for yourself more, have more clarity about your path in life, and improve your ability make lasting changes, large and small.

HOW TO USE THIS JOURNAL

There is something transformative about using hands to express our feelings, thoughts and emotions, and this is what we will be exploring throughout this journal.

The mere act of using our hands to express our inner world is grounding, and allows for body-mind-heart integration. It slows us down, bringing us into a more relaxed and balanced state of flow, where we can access deeper levels of our human experience. It's not just writing or coloring. It's an intimate process of connecting with our true self, as moods and emotions come right through on paper.

To make your journaling experience work best for you, set clear intentions and some basic guidelines.

1. Set aside time and space when you won't be interrupted for 20-30 minutes.
2. Pick your favorite pen and few colored pencils in colors you love.
3. Start with some movement to stir things up and get in touch with your body - do some yoga, stretch, dance or go for a short run.
4. Follow with a short meditation or grounding exercise to settle your mind and bring you into present awareness - sit for few minutes, open up to your senses and welcome in all sensations.
5. Write, color, or doodle freely – no shoulds or musts – express yourself completely from a place of spaciousness, compassion, and curiosity.
6. End with a brief meditation to facilitate self-reflection – observe your thoughts and feelings that have come up in journaling, allowing them to wash over you without judgment or attachment.

I open my heart, mind & life to change

THIS SPACE IS FOR

LOVE NOTE TO SELF * DOODLE * GRATITUDE CHECK IN

WHAT ARE YOU HOPING TO ACCOMPLISH WITH THIS JOURNAL? WHAT ARE YOU MAIN STRUGGLES THAT YOU ARE SEEKING TO OVERCOME? HOW DO YOU THINK JOURNALING WILL HELP YOU BECOME YOUR BEST SELF?

- to gain the confidence to move on w/ no plan
- the faith to not worry
- An appreciation of me & my intuition
- A vision of how to live successfully in a foreign country
- No depression or Anxiety
- Clarity on how to make $ Writing
- A New plan to find A new career.

LIVING INTENTIONALLY

Before we go deeper, we need to set an intention to be mindful, curious and open on this journey. To trust and let go. To be patient and persistent. To release the grip of habitual, knee-jerk reactions, whether it is negativity, anxiety or judgment, and instead become a curious observer and mindful creator of your life. Starting now.

Intentions are a fantastic way to help us stay grounded and reconnect with what matters most. They bring meaning and purposeful direction to all that we embark on.

Whenever we feel off balance, stressed out, or simply need guidance, we can call our intentions to the center of our mind, bring them back into focus. This centers and aligns us with what's important for us, allowing us to be congruent with our self in an authentic way.

Intentions are not goals, we don't work towards them. We already have all we need. We already embody what we wish for ourselves. Intentions help us reconnect with that knowing.

Your actions are always guided by intention, whether we set them consciously, or they are coming from the unconscious, often sabotaging our efforts. Becoming clear on our intentions allows us to live more purposely, mindfully, and in alignment with who we truly are.

Nourish and affirm your intentions with patience, persistence, perseverance, and love, and they will become the cornerstone of positive change in your life.

WRITE DOWN 3-5 DEEPEST DESIRES FOR YOURSELF AND YOUR LIFE. REREAD YOUR RESPONSES AND NOTICE HOW TRUE EACH FEELS ON AN INTUITIVE LEVEL IN YOUR BODY. DOES IT FEEL "RIGHT" IN YOUR GUT OR HEART AND NOT JUST IN YOUR THINKING MIND? CIRCLE KEYWORDS OR PHRASES THAT RESONATE WITH YOU THE MOST. THEN EXPRESS EACH INTENTION AS A CONCISE STATEMENT IN THE PRESENT TENSE, AS IF IT'S ALREADY TRUE. CLOSE YOUR EYES AND IMAGINE YOUR DESIRES ALREADY HAPPENING NOW. USE ALL YOUR SENSES TO VISUALIZE HOW THAT FEELS.

THIS SPACE IS FOR

LOVE NOTE TO SELF * DOODLE * GRATITUDE CHECK IN

PRACTICING AWARENESS

MINDFULNESS OPENS THE DOOR

Mindfulness opens the door to choosing – and changing – how we want to live in any given moment. Mindfulness, the state of open and non-judgmental awareness of what is, here and now, teaches us to observe what's happening within us and around us. Instead of getting hijacked by our often fear-driven thoughts and emotions, we notice them knowing they will eventually pass, then respond authentically, instead of reacting habitually.

There are many benefits to mindfulness we will embrace on our journey. Mindfulness is a perfect tool for deepening self-awareness, developing clarity and insight, unmasking self-defeating patterns and habitual behaviors, embracing pain with compassion and perspective, and fully experiencing the world as is, with all the beauty we would have otherwise missed because of the negativity bias built into the brain. Slowly, we can learn to become more awake to life's small pleasures, dropping chronic worry and endless distractions from taking over our lives. We can develop the freedom to think and act differently, build new habits, new mindset, new life.

Mindfulness brings awareness of our body, mind, and soul. With practice, we can use mindfulness to change how we react to life. We can train ourselves to get unstuck from a vicious cycle of negative thinking and habitual behavior. Instead of trying to control the outcome, we learn to flow with life as it unfolds. Instead of reacting from our habitual patterns rooted in fear and past wounds, we learn to respond with authenticity and compassion. With the shift in mindset, the way we live our life shifts.

5-STEP MINDFULNESS MEDITATION PRACTICE TO DEVELOP AWARENESS, ACCEPTANCE, AND COMPASSION

1. INTENTION

   Find a quiet and peaceful space for your meditation practice. Get comfortable, close your eyes gently, relax your body, consciously softening any obvious tension. Let go of any habitual thoughts or plans. Set an intention to be kind and loving to yourself. Decide to be gentle with yourself, offer compassion if anything difficult comes up.

2. BREATH

   Take a deep breath in, then release it slowly and completely. Then again, and again, stretching the first few in and out breaths. Slowly allow the breath to settle at your natural pace. Observe it as it flows in and out of your body. Feel the sensations of your breath carefully, relaxing into each breath. After a few breaths your mind will probably wander. When you notice this, gently guide your awareness back to your breath. Bring yourself back as many times as you wander off - this returning to your breath is the how you build your mindfulness muscle.

3. BODY

   Move your awareness into your physical body. Scan it slowly and notice any sensations: pleasant, unpleasant, and neutral. Is there tension, pain, heaviness, or restlessness? See if you can allow yourself to feel those sensations without trying to change them. Observe your sensations and allow them to pass.

4. MIND

   Notice any thoughts and feelings as they come up. Observe them and let them pass, like clouds in the sky. Try not to judge them, make them right or wrong, or allow them to take over this moment - just observe them as they come and go. Try to be present to any pain or discomfort that comes up - physical or emotional - not resist or fight it, but accept it is happening knowing that it will pass. If you start feeling overwhelmed, come back to the sensation of your breath. Feel it fully, moving in and out. Be gentle with yourself - this is hard work.

5. RELEASE

   Take a deep breath, scan your body again and release any tension you're still holding onto. Breathe in peace, breathe out tension (it's helpful to make some noise). Breathe in love and compassion, breathe out fear and pain. Let it all go. You are here now. Focus on something good in your life right now. Realize that good and bad are both present in every day but you can choose to focus on joy and gratitude. Breathe deeply, and thank yourself for being here.

THIS SPACE IS FOR

LOVE NOTE TO SELF * DOODLE * GRATITUDE CHECK IN

I observe & ride out all thoughts & emotions

THIS SPACE IS FOR

LOVE NOTE TO SELF * DOODLE * GRATITUDE CHECK IN

AFTER YOU'VE COMPLETED YOUR MINDFULNESS MEDITATION PRACTICE JOURNAL ABOUT THE EXPERIENCE. WHAT WAS IT LIKE FOR YOU? WAS IT HARD TO BE STILL? DID YOU GET LOST IN THOUGHT? WERE YOU ABLE TO COME BACK TO THE PRESENT MOMENT? WHAT REACTIONS AND "STORIES" HAVE COME UP? WHAT FEELINGS SHOWED UP? WHAT TRIGGERS HAVE YOU NOTICED? GIVE YOURSELF COMPASSION FOR GOING THROUGH THIS EXPERIENCE. OFFER YOURSELF KINDNESS AND GRATITUDE FOR SHOWING UP.

WHAT DOES IT MEAN TO BE PRESENT IN LIFE, TO LIVE MINDFULLY? WHAT DOES LIVING ON AUTOPILOT LOOK LIKE FOR YOU? ON A TYPICAL DAY, DO YOU MOSTLY LIVE IN THE PRESENT MOMENT, OR ARE YOU LOST IN THOUGHTS AND PAST/FUTURE EVENTS, HURTS, OR FEARS?

TO BE PRESENT IN LIFE YOU NEED TO BE PRESENT WITH YOURSELF FIRST. HOW DO YOU RECHARGE AND TAKE CARE OF YOURSELF? WHAT THINGS, BIG OR SMALL, DO YOU DO TO GET IN TOUCH WITH YOURSELF? WHICH ACTIVITIES FEEL GOOD AND MOST NATURAL TO YOU?

WHAT IS THE BIGGEST SOURCE OF STRESS IN YOUR LIFE RIGHT NOW? WHAT OR WHO TRIGGERS YOU MOST OFTEN?

WHAT IS YOUR HABITUAL RESPONSE TO STRESS? WHAT DO YOU DO, THINK OR REACH FOR WHEN YOU ARE OVERWHELMED? HOW DO YOU ESCAPE, NUMB OR DISTRACT YOURSELF FROM YOUR PAIN IN TIMES OF STRESS? WHAT STORY DO YOU TELL YOURSELF ABOUT YOUR ABILITY TO HANDLE STRESS & DIFFICULTY? WHAT BELIEFS DO YOU BUY INTO? HAVE YOU EVER CHALLENGED THOSE BELIEFS?

- Anger
- Reminiscation
- Depression
- Sadness
- Crying

THIS SPACE IS FOR

LOVE NOTE TO SELF * DOODLE * GRATITUDE CHECK IN

I treat myself with loving kindness & compassion

THIS SPACE IS FOR

LOVE NOTE TO SELF * DOODLE * GRATITUDE CHECK IN

WHAT SMALL CHANGE CAN YOU MAKE TO MINIMIZE THE LEVEL OF STRESS YOU ARE EXPERIENCING ON A DAILY BASIS? WHAT HABITS WOULD BRING IN PEACE, RECONNECT YOU WITH YOUR BODY, MIND, AND HEART? WHAT SMALL CHANGE WOULD SHIFT YOUR MOOD, YOUR ENERGY, YOUR DAY?

10 BODY BALANCING & HEALING HABITS

- Nourishing sleep and regular rest
- Exercise and rhythmic movement (swimming, jogging, dancing)
- Hydration and healthy nutrition
- Acupuncture, massage and healing touch (hugs, cuddles)
- Body scan and progressive muscle relaxation
- Grounding (breath, gardening, walking barefoot)
- Yoga, Tai Chi, and somatic experiencing
- Deep breathing and alternate nostril breathing
- Chakra clearing/balancing
- Detoxifying, juicing, and cleansing

10 MIND BALANCING & HEALING HABITS

- Meditation
- Mindfulness
- Journaling
- Positive attitude and optimism
- Fun and play
- Reading and learning
- Emotional healing work
- Self-compassion
- Healthy boundaries
- Emotional Freedom Technique (EFT)

10 HEART BALANCING & HEALING HABITS

- Gratitude, joy and laughter
- Being in nature
- Creativity and self-expression
- Nurturing relationships
- Self-acceptance and self-love
- Solitude
- Positive affirmations
- Visualizations
- Passions and hobbies
- Volunteering and giving

LOOKING AT THE BODY-MIND-HEART BALANCING AND HEALING HABITS LIST, CHECK OFF THE THINGS YOU ARE ALREADY DOING. WHICH HABITS COME NATURALLY, AND WHICH HABITS DO YOU HAVE TO PUSH YOURSELF TO DO? ARE YOU NOTICING ANY PATTERNS? WHICH PART OF YOUR SELF NEEDS MOST ATTENTION TODAY: BODY, MIND, OR HEART? WHAT NEW SELF-CARE HABIT CAN YOU COMMIT TO DOING TODAY, THIS WEEK, THIS MONTH, THIS YEAR?

WHAT BRINGS YOU BACK TO YOUR PHYSICAL BODY, HERE IN THE MOMENT? WHAT ARE THE BIGGEST OBSTACLES STANDING IN THE WAY OF FEELING CONNECTED AND AT HOME WITH YOUR BODY? WHAT CAN YOU DO TODAY TO HONOR AND TAKE CARE OF YOUR BODY?

WHEN IT COMES TO DAILY STRESS, HOW ARE YOUR SLEEPING AND EATING HABITS HELPING OR HINDERING THE HEALTH OF YOUR BODY? WHAT CHANGES DO YOU NEED TO MAKE TODAY TO SUPPORT YOURSELF MORE IN THIS AREA?

THIS SPACE IS FOR

LOVE NOTE TO SELF * DOODLE * GRATITUDE CHECK IN

I am beautiful and I am enough

THIS SPACE IS FOR

LOVE NOTE TO SELF * DOODLE * GRATITUDE CHECK IN

SIT STILL FOR FEW MINUTES WITH YOUR EYES CLOSED. LISTEN TO YOUR BODY AND BECOME CURIOUS. WHAT DOES YOUR BODY FEEL LIKE RIGHT NOW? WHAT IS IT LIKE TO BE IN YOUR SKIN? DO YOU FEEL HEAVY OR LIGHT, EXPANDED OR CONTRACTED, SOFT OR HARD, WARM OR COLD, TENSE OR PEACEFUL? IS THERE ANY PRESSURE, TINGLING, OR ITCHING? WHAT IS THE TEXTURE, WEIGHT, AND SHAPE OF SENSATIONS YOU NOTICE IN YOUR BODY. WHAT EMOTIONS ARE THOSE SENSATIONS CONNECTED TO? CAN YOU BREATHE INTO THE PARTS THAT CALL YOUR ATTENTION? WHAT DO THOSE PARTS OF YOUR BODY WANT TO TELL YOU?

DEEP BREATHING, THAT IS BREATHING DEEPLY INTO YOUR ABDOMINAL SPACE, STIMULATES THE VAGUS NERVE, SIGNALING THE BODY TO TURN ON THE PARASYMPATHETIC SYSTEM – OUR BUILT-IN RELAXATION RESPONSE WHICH PROMOTES THE STATE OF CALM AND HEALING.

LIE DOWN AND CLOSE YOUR EYES FOR FEW MINUTES. TAKE FEW DEEP, LONG BREATHS: INHALE THROUGH YOUR NOSE TO THE COUNT OF 2, PAUSE FOR ONE COUNT, THEN EXHALE THROUGH YOUR MOUTH TO THE COUNT OF 4 AND PAUSE FOR ONE COUNT. GO SLOW. PRACTICE DAILY FOR FEW MINUTES.

HOW DO YOU FEEL DURING AND AFTER THIS EXERCISE? IS YOUR BREATHING DEEP OR SHALLOW? ARE YOU RELAXED OR ANXIOUS WHILE BREATHING THIS WAY? NOTICE WHAT INHALATION AND EXHALATION FEELS LIKE IN YOUR NECK, THROAT, RIB CAGE, ABDOMEN, CHEST AND SHOULDERS. THIS SIMPLE ACT OF NOTICING EXPANSION HELPS US TUNE INTO WHO WE ARE.

SPENDING TIME IN NATURE CAN REDUCE STRESS, BRING CLARITY, AND NOURISH US PHYSICALLY, EMOTIONALLY, AND SPIRITUALLY. WHAT IS YOUR RELATIONSHIP WITH THE NATURAL WORLD? HOW ARE YOU CONNECTED WITH OR DISCONNECTED FROM NATURE ON A DAILY BASIS? WHAT OUTDOOR ACTIVITIES DO YOU ENJOY THE MOST? DO YOU GARDEN, HIKE, SPEND TIME NEAR WATER, OR SIMPLY ENJOY BIRDS SINGING WHILE YOU SIP YOUR MORNING COFFEE? HOW OFTEN DO YOU IMMERSE YOURSELF IN NATURE EXPERIENCING IT THROUGH SOUNDS, SMELLS, TOUCH, OR SIGHT? WHICH OF THE NATURAL ELEMENTS (AIR, FIRE, WATER, EARTH) DO YOU FEEL MOST DRAWN TO?

HOW CAN YOU INTENTIONALLY NURTURE JOY AND PLEASURE? HOW CAN YOU DEDICATE TO PLAYING AND HAVING FUN? WHAT ARE THREE THINGS YOU CAN DO TODAY THAT WILL NOURISH YOU AND BRING YOU JOY?

HEALING IS A CHOICE

WRITE THE HISTORY OF YOUR LIFE.

I gently untangle all my mental knots

THIS SPACE IS FOR

LOVE NOTE TO SELF * DOODLE * GRATITUDE CHECK IN

WRITE A LETTER TO YOURSELF AS A CHILD OR ADOLESCENT – PICK A TIME IN YOUR LIFE WHEN SOMETHING WAS DIFFICULT, WHEN YOU WERE STRUGGLING. WITHOUT JUDGEMENT OR AGENDA, NOTICE AND DESCRIBE YOUR INTERNAL REACTIONS AS YOU ARE THINKING ABOUT YOUR CHILDHOOD. WHAT EMOTIONS AND SENSATIONS COME UP?

WHAT DID YOU NOT GET AS A CHILD THAT YOU ARE NOW SEEKING AS AN ADULT? WHAT EMOTIONS COME UP WHEN YOU ARE THINKING/WRITING ABOUT THIS? LET YOURSELF EXPERIENCE YOUR PAIN BRIEFLY. BE PRESENT TO IT WITHOUT JUDGEMENT AND WITH COMPASSION FOR YOUR SUFFERING. WHAT DOES YOUR BODY FEEL LIKE RIGHT NOW? IS THERE ANY PAIN? WHERE IS THAT HURT LOCATED? BREATHE LOVE INTO THAT SPACE, WATCH IT PASS LIKE CLOUDS IN THE SKY.

IF YOU START TO GET OVERWHELMED, PAUSE, PLACE A HAND OVER YOUR HEART AND TAKE FEW DEEP BREATHS. FOCUS ON THE SENSATION OF YOUR BREATH GOING IN AND OUT. LISTEN TO IT TRAVEL THROUGH YOUR BODY. FEEL IT AS IT FLOWS THROUGH YOUR MOUTH AND NOSE. SIT STILL UNTIL THE STORM PASSES.

WHAT DID YOU LEARN IN YOUR FAMILY GROWING UP ON HOW TO HANDLE CONFLICT, MOMENTS OF DISCOMFORT OR STRUGGLE?

HOW WAS ANGER EXPRESSED (OR REPRESSED) IN YOUR FAMILY? HOW DO YOU EXPRESS ANGER AS AN ADULT? DO YOU REPRESS ANGER SOMETIMES, OFTEN, OR CHRONICALLY? WHEN? WITH WHOM? WHY? HOW ARE YOU GIVING POWER AWAY WITH OFFENSIVE ANGER? IN WHAT SITUATIONS DO YOU "LOSE IT", REACT, ATTACK OR BLAME? WHERE IS ANGER LOCATED IN YOUR BODY? BREATHE INTO THAT SPACE. WHAT DOES IT FEEL LIKE?

WHAT IS HAPPENING IN YOUR LIFE RIGHT NOW THAT YOU WISH YOU COULD CHANGE? WHAT IS THE BIGGEST SOURCE OF FRUSTRATION? WHAT IS THE SOURCE OF YOUR ANGER? WHAT BOUNDARIES ARE BEING PUSHED OR CROSSED? WHAT NEEDS ARE NOT BEING MET?

THIS SPACE IS FOR

LOVE NOTE TO SELF * DOODLE * GRATITUDE CHECK IN

I let my inner wisdom & intuition guide me

THIS SPACE IS FOR

LOVE NOTE TO SELF * DOODLE * GRATITUDE CHECK IN

WHAT ARE YOUR NON-NEGOTIABLE NEEDS IN INTIMATE RELATIONSHIPS?

HOW ARE YOU NOT HONORING YOURSELF AND YOUR NEEDS? IN WHAT SITUATIONS DO YOU SAY "YES" WHEN YOU REALLY MEAN "NO"? HOW ARE YOU NOT RESPECTING YOURSELF AND YOUR BOUNDARIES?

MAKE A LIST OF YOUR MOST IMPORTANT NEEDS AND DESIRES. HOW CAN YOU ASK FOR YOUR NEEDS TO BE MET? HOW CAN YOU MEET THEM FOR YOURSELF?

WHAT DOES THE CHILD WITHIN YOU NEED RIGHT NOW? WHAT PART OF YOU MOST NEEDS YOUR ATTENTION, LOVE AND COMPASSION? HOW CAN YOU GIVE YOURSELF THE NURTURING AND CARE YOUR INNER CHILD CRAVES?

IS THERE ANYTHING YOU CAN'T LET GO OF BUT YOU KNOW YOU NEED TO? HOW CAN YOU FACE WHAT YOU NEED TO FACE IN ORDER TO HEAL AND GROW?

THIS SPACE IS FOR

LOVE NOTE TO SELF * DOODLE * GRATITUDE CHECK IN

I release the pain of the past

THIS SPACE IS FOR

LOVE NOTE TO SELF * DOODLE * GRATITUDE CHECK IN

WHO IN YOUR LIFE DO YOU NEED TO FORGIVE?

WHAT DO YOU WORRY ABOUT THE MOST? WHAT ARE YOU TOP FIVE FEARS? BEGINNING WITH YOUR LEAST POWERFUL FEAR AND GOING DOWN THE LIST ONE BY ONE, ASK YOURSELF: WHY DOES IT MAKE YOU FEARFUL? WHAT WOULD HAPPEN IF THAT FEAR CAME TRUE? WHY ARE YOU AFRAID OF THAT OUTCOME? WHAT IS THE WORST THING THAT COULD HAPPEN? HOW MUCH POWER ARE YOU ALLOWING THIS FEAR TO HAVE OVER YOUR LIFE?

HOW ARE YOU SELF-SACRIFICING AND MAKING YOURSELF INVISIBLE? ARE YOU HIDING BEHIND BUSYNESS AND MARTYRDOM? WHAT ARE YOU AFRAID OF?

HOW DO YOUR FEARS DETERMINE YOUR SELF-CONCEPT, SELF-IMAGE, SELF-ESTEEM? HOW DO THESE FEARS INHIBIT YOU, STOP YOU FROM MAKING A CHANGE IN YOUR LIFE, KEEP YOU CHAINED DOWN, SMALL AND UNFULFILLED? WHAT WOULD YOUR LIFE LOOK LIKE WITHOUT THOSE FEARS?

WHAT NEW BEHAVIORS DO YOU NEED TO DEVELOP IN ORDER TO CONFRONT YOUR FEARS? WHAT LIMITING BELIEFS ARE IN THE WAY? WHAT CHILDHOOD PROGRAMS ARE BLOCKING YOUR PROGRESS? WHAT NEGATIVE CORE BELIEFS ABOUT YOURSELF AND THE WORLD FUEL YOUR FEARS?

THIS SPACE IS FOR

LOVE NOTE TO SELF * DOODLE * GRATITUDE CHECK IN

I allow shift to unravel

THIS SPACE IS FOR

LOVE NOTE TO SELF * DOODLE * GRATITUDE CHECK IN

HOW ARE YOU CONTROLLING IN YOUR LIFE RIGHT NOW? WHAT ARE YOU AFRAID OF THAT IS DRIVING YOU TO CONTROL? IS YOUR FEAR REALISTIC? CAN YOU ACTUALLY CONTROL IT? IS IT WORTH LOOSING PEACE AND INTIMACY OVER IT? WHERE IS CONTROL LOCATED IN YOUR BODY? OBSERVE IT, AND BREATHE INTO THAT SPACE. WHAT DOES IT FEEL LIKE?

DO YOU HAVE A HABIT OF TRYING TO PLEASE EVERYONE ALL OF THE TIME? WHAT PURPOSE DOES THIS SERVE YOU? WHAT FEAR HOLDS YOU BACK FROM SPEAKING YOUR TRUTH?

WHAT SELF-DEFEATING HABITS DO YOU NEED TO BREAK?

DESCRIBE THE WAYS IN WHICH YOU CREATE DISTANCE IN RELATIONSHIPS. WHAT NEGATIVE PATTERNS DO YOU KEEP REPEATING IN YOUR MOST INTIMATE RELATIONSHIPS?

WHAT ARE YOU BELIEVING ABOUT YOURSELF THAT IS CREATING SUFFERING RIGHT NOW? WHAT SELF-DEFEATING STORIES HAVE YOU BEEN TELLING YOURSELF ABOUT YOU AND YOUR PLACE IN THE WORLD THAT ARE CREATING PAIN AND STOPPING YOU FROM FULLY EXPERIENCING LIFE? FEEL INTO THAT HURT PLACE IN YOURSELF, AND SURROUND IT WITH LOVE AND COMPASSION. NOTICE THE SHAPE, TEMPERATURE, TEXTURE OF YOUR PAIN.

THIS SPACE IS FOR

LOVE NOTE TO SELF * DOODLE * GRATITUDE CHECK IN

I let go of all fears & worry

THIS SPACE IS FOR

LOVE NOTE TO SELF * DOODLE * GRATITUDE CHECK IN

WHAT DO YOU FEEL GUILTY ABOUT MOST? WHAT STOPS YOU FROM FORGIVING YOURSELF? LET YOURSELF EXPERIENCE THAT GUILT BRIEFLY. BE PRESENT TO IT WITHOUT JUDGEMENT AND WITH COMPASSION FOR YOUR SUFFERING. WHAT DOES IT FEEL LIKE IN YOUR BODY? WHAT DOES IT LOOK LIKE? WHERE IS IT LOCATED? BREATHE INTO THAT SPACE FEELING IT FULLY.

IN WHAT AREAS OF YOUR LIFE DOES NEGATIVE SELF-TALK COME UP THE MOST FOR YOU? WHAT DO YOU BELIEVE ABOUT YOURSELF THAT IS FUELING THAT INNER DIALOG?

THINK ABOUT HOW YOU TALKED TO YOURSELF TODAY. TUNE INTO THAT INTERNAL DIALOG RIGHT NOW. WAS IT ENCOURAGING OR DEFEATING, UPLIFTING OR CRITICAL? TUNE INTO YOUR BODY AND BREATHE INTO ANY AREAS THAT FEEL TIGHT OR TRIGGERED. NOTICE ANY SENSATIONS AS THEY COME AND GO. ALLOW THEM TO PASS. WHEN YOU ARE DONE, WRITE DOWN POSITIVE COUNTER-MESSAGES FOR EVERY NEGATIVE MESSAGE YOU HAVE TOLD YOURSELF TODAY.

WHEN YOU ARE OVERWHELMED OR ASHAMED, HOW DO YOU NUMB YOUR FEELINGS? DO YOU FIGHT, RUN OR HIDE? WHAT FEELING ARE YOU AVOIDING/DENYING?

I am gentle with myself

THIS SPACE IS FOR

LOVE NOTE TO SELF * DOODLE * GRATITUDE CHECK IN

WHAT DOES YOUR INNER CRITIC SAY TO YOU WHEN YOU LOOK IN THE MIRROR, WHEN YOU GET DRESSED, WHEN YOU COME TO A PARTY WHERE YOU DON'T KNOW MANY PEOPLE, WHEN YOU COME UP WITH A BIG IDEA, WHEN YOU TRY TO RECLAIM A CREATIVE HOBBY, WHEN YOU TAKE TIME FOR YOURSELF, WHEN YOU ARE FEELING CHALLENGED AS A PARTNER OR A PARENT? WHAT BELIEFS ARE YOU HOLDING ONTO AND WHY? WHAT CAN YOU RELEASE TODAY?

WRITE ABOUT A SITUATION IN YOUR LIFE WHEN YOU JUDGED YOURSELF HARSHLY FOR A MISTAKE YOU'VE MADE, BIG OR SMALL. HOW DID YOU FEEL ABOUT YOURSELF THEN? WHAT DOES IT FEEL LIKE IN YOUR BODY WHEN YOU CRITICISE AND BERATE YOURSELF? NOTICE ANY TIGHTNESS OR PLACES THAT FEEL HEAVY, SOLID, HOT. BREATHE LOVE AND COMPASSION INTO THOSE AREAS, LETTING ANY SENSATION MOVE THROUGH YOUR BODY. NOW, BRING UP A SITUATION WHEN INSTEAD OF SELF-LOATHING YOU OFFERED YOURSELF COMPASSION AND KINDNESS, OR IMAGINE YOURSELF DOING THAT. HOW DIFFERENT IS YOUR INTERNAL EXPERIENCE?

BRING TO MIND SOME DIFFICULTY YOU ARE GOING THROUGH IN YOUR LIFE RIGHT NOW. NOTICE THE PAIN, DISAPPOINTMENT, FEAR, GRIEF, FRUSTRATION OR WHATEVER ELSE YOU MAY FEEL AROUND THIS DIFFICULT SITUATION. ACKNOWLEDGE TO YOURSELF, "THIS IS A MOMENT OF SUFFERING. ALL HUMANS EXPERIENCE MOMENTS OF SUFFERING." REPEAT UNTIL IT FEELS INTERNALIZED. THEN ASK YOURSELF WHERE IN YOUR BODY THIS SUFFERING IS BEING STORED. PUT YOUR HANDS THERE, DRAWING OUR ATTENTION TO THAT SPACE. FEEL IT FULLY, IMAGINING THE ENERGY OF THAT SPACE. NOURISH THAT PART OF YOUR BODY WITH YOUR BREATH FOR AS LONG AS YOU LIKE. WRITE DOWN ANY THOUGHTS, FEELINGS, EMOTIONS AND SENSATIONS THAT CAME UP.

IF YOUR FRIEND EXPRESSED FEELINGS OF SELF-DOUBT AND WAS SELF-CRITICAL, WHAT WOULD YOU TELL THEM?

HOW CAN YOU GIVE YOURSELF THE REASSURANCE YOU NEED WHEN THINGS ARE HARD? WHAT CAN YOU TELL YOURSELF? HOW CAN YOU SOOTHE YOUR WORRIES?

THIS SPACE IS FOR

LOVE NOTE TO SELF * DOODLE * GRATITUDE CHECK IN

I invite all feelings to guide me

THIS SPACE IS FOR

LOVE NOTE TO SELF * DOODLE * GRATITUDE CHECK IN

WRITE DOWN 10 WAYS IN WHICH YOU ARE NOT BEING VERY LOVING TO YOURSELF. HOW CAN YOU BE MORE CARING AND SUPPORTIVE INSTEAD?

HOW HAVE YOU BEEN ABANDONING YOURSELF? HOW HAVE YOU BEEN TUNING YOUR FEELINGS OUT WITH YOUR MIND, YOUR ADDICTIONS, SELF-CRITICISM, BLAME, PEOPLE PLEASING, PERFECTIONISM, TAKING CARE OF EVERYONE BUT YOURSELF?

WHEN DO YOU FEEL REJECTED, IGNORED OR UNSEEN MOST? WITH WHOM? WHAT ARE YOU WANTING TO HEAR FROM THEM THAT YOU CAN TELL YOURSELF?

SIT QUIETLY FOR FEW MINUTES AND FOCUS YOUR ATTENTION ON THE WORD "TRUST". RECALL A PERSON WHOM YOU TRUST, THEN THINK OF SOMEONE YOU DON'T TRUST. WHERE DOES TRUST AND DISTRUST EXIST IN YOUR BODY? BREATHE INTO THOSE AREAS NOTICING ANY PATTERNS AND SENSATIONS.

IN WHAT WAYS HAVE YOU NOT BEEN TRUSTING YOURSELF?

THIS SPACE IS FOR

LOVE NOTE TO SELF * DOODLE * GRATITUDE CHECK IN

I am worthy of love & belonging

THIS SPACE IS FOR

LOVE NOTE TO SELF * DOODLE * GRATITUDE CHECK IN

WHAT DO YOU DISLIKE MOST ABOUT YOURSELF? WHICH IMPERFECTIONS MAKE YOU FEEL INADEQUATE? WHAT WOULD HAPPEN IF YOU LOVED EVERY SINGLE ONE OF YOUR FLAWS OR FAILURES. HOW WOULD YOUR LIFE BE DIFFERENT? HOW WOULD THE LIVES OF PEOPLE AROUND YOU CHANGE? AS YOU WRITE, NOTICE THE PAIN OF SELF-JUDGEMENT STORED IN YOUR BODY AND OFFER YOURSELF COMPASSION BREATHING TENDERNESS INTO THAT SPACE.

WHAT DO YOU NEED TO START ACCEPTING ABOUT YOUR BODY, YOUR PERSONALITY, AND YOUR PERCEIVED WEAKNESSES? WHAT SELF-TALK DO YOU NEED TO CHANGE TO START THIS PROCESS? WRITE DOWN POSITIVE AFFIRMATIONS THAT WILL REPLACE SELF-CRITICAL THOUGHTS YOU HAVE ABOUT YOURSELF.

NOTICE THE THINGS YOU SAY TO YOURSELF ON A REGULAR BASIS. DO THEY SERVE YOU OR HOLD YOU BACK? WHAT NEGATIVE BELIEFS AND THOUGHT PATTERNS ABOUT YOURSELF DO YOU NEED TO DROP?

WHO SPEAKS NEGATIVELY TO YOU? WHO REINFORCES YOUR NEGATIVE SELF-TALK? HOW HAVE YOU ADOPTED THEIR JUDGEMENT AS YOUR OWN? HOW CAN YOU BEGIN LETTING THOSE SELF-DEFEATING STORIES GO? WHAT DO YOU WANT TO BELIEVE ABOUT YOURSELF INSTEAD?

WHAT ARE YOU BLAMING YOURSELF FOR? WHAT DO YOU HEAR YOUR JUDGING SELF SAY ABOUT YOU? WHERE IS BLAME LOCATED IN YOUR BODY? HOW DOES IT FEEL?

THIS SPACE IS FOR

LOVE NOTE TO SELF * DOODLE * GRATITUDE CHECK IN

I release stuck energy, old habits & expectations

THIS SPACE IS FOR

LOVE NOTE TO SELF * DOODLE * GRATITUDE CHECK IN

WHAT PAST MISTAKES AND FAILURES ARE YOU DESPERATELY HOLDING ONTO? WHY ARE YOU REFUSING TO LET THEM GO? WHAT DO YOU NEED TO DO IN ORDER TO RELEASE THEM?

WHAT EXPECTATIONS HAVE YOU BEEN PUTTING ON YOURSELF THAT ARE MAKING YOU MISERABLE? WHAT EXPECTATIONS AROUND PARENTING OR RELATIONSHIPS ARE YOU WILLING TO RELEASE?

HOW CAN YOU START SEEING, ATTENDING TO, AND ACCEPTING YOURSELF MORE?

WHAT CAN YOU DO FOR YOURSELF EACH DAY TO MAKE YOU FEEL MORE BEAUTIFUL, SMART, CREATIVE?

CLOSE YOUR EYES AND REMEMBER A TIME WHEN YOU ACCOMPLISHED SOMETHING GREAT, MEANINGFUL OR DIFFICULT. RE-LIVE HOW IT FELT TO SUCCEED. FEEL IT IN YOUR BODY. WHAT DID COURAGE AND MOTIVATION FEEL LIKE THEN? HOW CAN YOU TAP INTO THAT INNER STRENGTH MORE OFTEN? WHAT ACTIVITIES CAN YOU DO DAILY TO STRENGTHEN THOSE QUALITIES?

THIS SPACE IS FOR

LOVE NOTE TO SELF * DOODLE * GRATITUDE CHECK IN

All I need is already within me

THIS SPACE IS FOR

LOVE NOTE TO SELF * DOODLE * GRATITUDE CHECK IN

WRITE ABOUT A TIME THAT YOU HAVE FELT VULNERABLE. WHAT DOES THE WORD 'VULNERABILITY' MEAN TO YOU? WHAT DOES VULNERABILITY FEEL LIKE OR LOOK LIKE TO YOU?

HOW DID YOU SHOW COMPASSION FOR YOURSELF THIS WEEK?

WHAT DOES UNCONDITIONAL LOVE LOOK LIKE TO YOU? WHAT DOES UNCONDITIONAL SELF-LOVE LOOK LIKE?

THIS SPACE IS FOR

LOVE NOTE TO SELF * DOODLE * GRATITUDE CHECK IN

I choose what honors & supports me

THIS SPACE IS FOR

LOVE NOTE TO SELF * DOODLE * GRATITUDE CHECK IN

WRITE A LETTER TO YOURSELF FROM A PERSPECTIVE OF A FRIEND WHO LOVES YOU UNCONDITIONALLY. READ THE LETTER SOME TIME LATER LETTING THE WORDS SINK IN. FEEL THE COMPASSION AS IT POURS INTO YOU. FEEL IT ENTERING YOUR BODY AS YOU BREATHE THE LOVE IN. LET IT SOOTHE AND COMFORT YOU.

LIST 10 WORDS THAT DESCRIBE YOU. HOW DO YOU FEEL IN YOUR BODY AS YOU MAKE THAT LIST?

HOW DO YOU MEASURE YOUR SELF-WORTH? DO YOU TIE IT TO YOUR ACCOMPLISHMENTS, LOOKS, CAREER, YOUR PERCEIVED POPULARITY, PARENTING ABILITIES, OR YOUR NET WORTH?

LIST 10 THINGS YOU LOVE ABOUT YOURSELF THAT HAVE NOTHING TO DO WITH ACHIEVEMENT.

HOW CAN YOU LOVE YOURSELF MORE? WHAT IS THE ONE THING YOU CAN COMMIT TO DOING DAILY FOR YOURSELF THAT WILL NOURISH AND RECHARGE YOU?

THIS SPACE IS FOR

LOVE NOTE TO SELF * DOODLE * GRATITUDE CHECK IN

I can only heal through loving myself

THIS SPACE IS FOR

LOVE NOTE TO SELF * DOODLE * GRATITUDE CHECK IN

MAKE A LIST OF PEOPLE IN YOUR LIFE WHO GENUINELY SUPPORT YOU, AND WHOM YOU CAN TRUST?

WHAT MISTAKES HAVE YOU MADE TODAY? HOW DO YOU FEEL ABOUT THAT? WHAT HAVE YOU LEARNED?

WHAT DOES SELF-ACCEPTANCE MEAN TO YOU? HOW DO YOU EMBRACE WHO YOU TRULY ARE WITH LOVE AND ACCEPTANCE, NO MATTER THE SITUATION?

REWRITE A STORY OF YOUR LIFE, BUT THIS TIME EMPHASIZE THE POSITIVE THINGS AND EVENTS, AND WHAT YOU HAVE LEARNED FROM THEM. CREATE THE PERSON YOU REALLY ARE NOW: ABLE TO MAKE NEW CHOICES, OVERCOME PAST PROBLEMS, ACCOMPLISH GOALS. YOU ARE NO LONGER A VICTIM, BUT YOUR OWN HERO. REWRITE YOUR STORY FROM A PLACE OF STRENGTH AND POWER.

CREATE YOUR OWN PATH

WHAT IS RIGHT IN YOUR LIFE? FOR WHAT IN YOUR LIFE DO YOU FEEL MOST GRATEFUL?

THINK ABOUT TIMES WHEN YOU FELT HAPPIEST. CONSIDER MOMENTS IN YOUR LIFE THAT FELT REALLY PRECIOUS TO YOU - SACRED MOMENTS, MOMENTS THAT REALLY MATTERED. WHAT WERE THOSE MOMENTS? LIST THE HAPPIEST MOMENTS OF YOUR LIFE.

LIST 20 SMALL AND EVERYDAY THINGS THAT MAKE YOU HAPPY AND BRING YOU JOY.

WHAT MAKES YOU FEEL HEALTHY, IN YOUR BODY, MIND, AND HEART?

THIS SPACE IS FOR

LOVE NOTE TO SELF * DOODLE * GRATITUDE CHECK IN

I am in charge of my own happiness

THIS SPACE IS FOR

LOVE NOTE TO SELF * DOODLE * GRATITUDE CHECK IN

WHEN WAS THE LAST TIME YOU FELT TRULY LIGHT, JOYOUS, AND HAPPY? WHEN WAS THE LAST TIME YOU CAME ALIVE? WHAT WERE YOU DOING? WHO WAS WITH YOU?

WHAT DID YOU LOVE DOING AS A CHILD THAT YOU NO LONGER DO? IS THERE ANYTHING THAT MAKES YOU FEEL LIKE TIME DOES NOT EXIST? IS THERE A CREATIVE SIDE OF YOU THAT HAS GONE UNDERGROUND? HOW CAN YOU RECLAIM IT?

HOW DID I FEEL THE LAST TIME I MADE SOMETHING BY HAND? HOW DO YOU FEEL WHEN YOU'RE CREATING? WHAT DOES CREATIVITY LOOK LIKE FOR YOU?

WHAT DO YOU BELIEVE ABOUT YOUR CREATIVE ABILITIES? ARE YOU BELIEFS LIMITING OR EMPOWERING?

WHAT DOES YOUR INNER CHILD NEED RIGHT NOW?

THIS SPACE IS FOR

LOVE NOTE TO SELF * DOODLE * GRATITUDE CHECK IN

I express myself freely & openly

THIS SPACE IS FOR

LOVE NOTE TO SELF * DOODLE * GRATITUDE CHECK IN

HOW DO YOU WANT TO FEEL TODAY, THIS MONTH, THIS YEAR?

WRITE IN A STREAM OF CONSCIOUSNESS FOR 5-10 MINUTES, STARTING WITH, "TODAY, I FEEL..." DON'T EDIT YOUR THOUGHTS OR FEELINGS, AND DON'T CORRECT YOUR GRAMMAR. THIS IS CENSOR-FREE WRITING.

WHAT WAS THE MOST MEANINGFUL EXPERIENCE YOU HAVE EVER HAD?

FINISH THE SENTENCE: WHEN I AM NOT DOING I AM...

WHAT IS MOST IMPORTANT TO YOU IN LIFE? WHAT IS A GOOD LIFE TO YOU? AT THE END OF YOUR LIFE, WHAT WILL TRULY MATTER?

THIS SPACE IS FOR

LOVE NOTE TO SELF * DOODLE * GRATITUDE CHECK IN

I'm free to choose my destiny

THIS SPACE IS FOR

LOVE NOTE TO SELF * DOODLE * GRATITUDE CHECK IN

WHAT MAKES YOU FEEL SAFE AND LOVED?

WHAT IS YOUR VERSION OF HAVING IT ALL?

WRITE A DETAILED DESCRIPTION OF WHAT YOU TRULY WANT.

HOW WOULD YOU FEEL IF YOU GOT WHAT YOU WANTED?

WHAT ARE SOME OF THE MOST IMPORTANT THINGS ABOUT YOU AS A PERSON? WHAT DO YOU VALUE THE MOST?

THIS SPACE IS FOR

LOVE NOTE TO SELF * DOODLE * GRATITUDE CHECK IN

I recognize my inner strength & power

THIS SPACE IS FOR

LOVE NOTE TO SELF * DOODLE * GRATITUDE CHECK IN

THINK BACK TO ALL THE TIMES WHEN YOU FELT TRULY FULFILLED, WHEN YOU FELT ALIVE AND MOTIVATED, WHEN YOU LOST TRACK OF TIME BECAUSE YOU WERE DOING SOMETHING YOU LOVED, WHEN YOU FELT MOST ENERGIZED AND ENGAGED. WHAT WERE YOU DOING? WHO WAS WITH YOU? HOW DID YOU FEEL?

WHEN OR WHERE DO YOU SHINE? IS THERE SOMETHING THAT YOU DO THAT SEEMS EFFORTLESS TO YOU? WHAT DO YOU DO REALLY WELL? WHAT ARE YOU NATURALLY GOOD AT? WHAT IS YOUR GENIUS? WHAT IS YOUR UNIQUENESS?

WHAT ARE YOU INTERESTED IN RIGHT NOW? WHAT ARE YOU CURIOUS ABOUT? WHAT MAKES YOU LIGHT UP WITH INTEREST, GET EXCITED? WHAT INSPIRES YOU?

WHAT ARE SOME OF THE THINGS YOU LOVED DOING AS A CHILD? WHAT ARE YOU NATURALLY DRAWN TO? WHAT DO YOU SPEND HOURS LEARNING ABOUT? WHAT SPARKS YOUR CURIOSITY? WHAT ARE YOU INTENSELY INTERESTED IN?

WHAT ARE YOU THREE GREATEST STRENGTHS? HOW CAN YOU LEVERAGE ALL THREE IN AN UNIQUE WAY? HOW CAN YOU ACTIVATE AND UTILIZE THEM MORE IN YOUR LIFE?

THIS SPACE IS FOR

LOVE NOTE TO SELF * DOODLE * GRATITUDE CHECK IN

I am responsible for my own life

THIS SPACE IS FOR

LOVE NOTE TO SELF * DOODLE * GRATITUDE CHECK IN

WHAT IS THE ONE THING YOU HAVE ALWAYS DREAMED ABOUT BUT NEVER GOT TO DO? IS THERE SOMETHING YOU'VE BEEN AFRAID TO TRY BECAUSE IT TAKES YOU OUT OF YOUR COMFORT ZONE?

HOW WOULD YOUR LIFE CHANGE IF YOU BELIEVED IN YOUR DREAMS AND WERE ABLE TO DO WHAT MAKES YOU HAPPY FOR A LIVING?

IF YOU KNEW THERE WAS NO WAY TO FAIL, WHAT WOULD YOU DO NEXT IN YOUR LIFE?

WHAT IS YOUR LIFE'S PURPOSE? HOW DO YOU WANT TO CONTRIBUTE TO THE WORLD? WHAT LEGACY DO YOU WANT TO LEAVE? WHAT DO YOU WANT TO BE KNOWN FOR?

WHAT WAS YOUR FIRST SIGNIFICANT ACHIEVEMENT? WHAT WAS THE SINGLE BIGGEST SUCCESS/ACCOMPLISHMENT YOU'VE EVER HAD IN YOUR LIFE?

THIS SPACE IS FOR

LOVE NOTE TO SELF * DOODLE * GRATITUDE CHECK IN

I have everything I need

THIS SPACE IS FOR

LOVE NOTE TO SELF * DOODLE * GRATITUDE CHECK IN

WHAT CHALLENGES YOU? WHAT ARE YOUR WEAKNESSES?

IF NO ONE JUDGED YOU, WHO WOULD YOU BE?

LIST 5 THINGS YOU ARE MOST PASSIONATE ABOUT. HOW CAN YOU MAKE ROOM FOR EACH IN YOUR DAILY LIFE?

WHAT KIND OF RELATIONSHIP WOULD YOU LIKE TO CREATE WITH YOURSELF, YOUR PARTNER, YOUR CHILDREN, YOUR PARENTS? WHAT CAN YOU DO TODAY (THIS MONTH, THIS YEAR) TO MOVE TOWARDS YOUR IDEAL RELATIONSHIPS?

WRITE OUT YOUR ENTIRE PERFECT DAY, FROM WAKING UP IN THE MORNING TILL THE MOMENT YOU FALL ASLEEP. DON'T LIMIT, CENSOR OR EDIT YOURSELF.

I claim my space in the world

THIS SPACE IS FOR

LOVE NOTE TO SELF * DOODLE * GRATITUDE CHECK IN

IMAGINE YOUR LIFE IN THE FUTURE (5, 10, 20 YEARS FROM NOW) AS IF YOU'VE ACHIEVED ALL YOUR GOALS. DREAM BIG. WHAT DOES YOUR LIFE LOOK LIKE? HOW DO YOU FEEL? WHAT HAVE YOU ACCOMPLISHED? HOW DID YOU GET THERE?

IF YOU WERE FREE TO CHOOSE, WHAT WOULD YOU BE DOING WITH YOUR LIFE RIGHT NOW?

WHERE WERE YOU IN YOUR LIFE AT THIS TIME LAST YEAR? IN WHAT AREAS HAVE YOU GROWN? WHERE DO YOU STILL NEED TO FOCUS ON CHANGE?

WHAT IS MISSING IN YOUR LIFE? WHAT ARE YOU HUNGRY FOR? HOW FULFILLED DO YOU FEEL IN YOUR LIFE RIGHT NOW? ARE YOU DOING WHAT YOU REALLY WANT TO DO?

IS THERE SOMETHING YOU'VE DREAMED OF DOING FOR A LONG TIME? WHY HAVEN'T YOU DONE IT? WHAT CALLING ARE YOU POSTPONING BECAUSE OF FEAR?

THIS SPACE IS FOR

LOVE NOTE TO SELF * DOODLE * GRATITUDE CHECK IN

I recognize & unleash my potential

THIS SPACE IS FOR

LOVE NOTE TO SELF * DOODLE * GRATITUDE CHECK IN

WHAT DO YOU MOST WANT RIGHT NOW? WHAT DO YOU NEED TO DO TO MOVE TOWARD EMOTIONAL FULFILLMENT? WHAT IS ONE ACTION YOU CAN TAKE TODAY TO MOVE FORWARD?

WHAT ARE YOU WILLING TO GIVE UP IN ORDER TO CREATE THE LIFE OF YOUR DREAMS?

WHAT IS THE ONE THING YOU CAN DO TODAY THAT WILL MOVE YOU CLOSER TO YOUR DREAM LIFE?

WHAT ARE YOUR TOP 5 GOALS IN LIFE? HOW ARE YOU SUPPORTING YOUR GOALS IN YOUR DAILY LIFE? WHAT DO YOU NEED TO MAKE MORE ROOM FOR?

HOW DO YOU WANT TO FEEL A YEAR FROM NOW? WHAT DO YOU NEED TO START/STOP DOING TO GET THERE?

THIS SPACE IS FOR

LOVE NOTE TO SELF * DOODLE * GRATITUDE CHECK IN

I have
the power to
choose

THIS SPACE IS FOR

LOVE NOTE TO SELF * DOODLE * GRATITUDE CHECK IN

DESCRIBE IN GREAT DETAIL WHAT YOUR IDEAL LIFE LOOKS LIKE. USE ALL YOUR SENSES TO MAKE YOUR VISION AS REAL AS POSSIBLE. MAKE THE DETAILS SO VIVID THAT YOU CAN ACTUALLY EXPERIENCE WHAT IT FEELS LIKE TO BE LIVING THAT LIFE RIGHT NOW.

ABOUT THE AUTHOR

Joanna Ciolek is a self-taught artist, recovering self-critic, and a firm believer in the healing and transformative powers of mindfulness. Born and raised in Poland, she now lives with her husband and three children in Denver, Colorado.

Made in the USA
San Bernardino, CA
21 June 2020

73815579R00124